IMAGES OF ENGLAND

AROUND

PORTHCAWL

NEWTON AND NOTTAGE

Porthcawl Dock in the heyday of the coal export trade, 1887. To the centre of the photograph are the massive lock gates. These were closed when the tide went out to ensure that a sufficient level of water was maintained in the inner basin.

IMAGES OF ENGLAND

AROUND
PORTHCAWL
NEWTON AND NOTTAGE

KEITH MORGAN

The History Press

This recently discovered photograph is possibly the oldest in existence of the Esplanade and Sea Bank House at Porthcawl. It has been dated to about 1885. Found by the Porthcawl Museum and Historical Society, the original is a 4-inch glass magic lantern slide which is both cracked and in very poor condition. Using modern computer digital imaging, the slide has been expertly reproduced and enhanced to enable a clear photographic image to be re-created. Sea Bank House, on the left of the photograph, was built by George Dement as New House about 1865 while construction of both the Esplanade, and the Esplanade Hotel on the right, was completed by 1887, the year of Queen Victoria's Golden Jubilee. Note the water carrier which was used to transport drinking water from Ffynnon Fawr, the well at Nottage.

First published in 1996 by Tempus Publishing
Reprinted 2000, 2004

Reprinted in 2008 by
The History Press
The Mill, Brimscombe Port,
Stroud, Gloucestershire, GL5 2QG
www.thehistorypress.co.uk

Reprinted 2017

British Library Cataloguing in Publication Data.
A catalogue record for this book is available from the British Library.

ISBN 978 0 7524 0607 7

Typesetting and origination by Tempus Publishing Limited.
Printed in Great Britain by TJ International Ltd, Padstow, Cornwall

This enchanting little photograph of a young girl with donkeys was taken at Nottage Court in 1887 and captioned: 'When shall we three meet again'.

Contents

Acknowledgements

This is the second book in the *Archives Photographs* series that I have had the privilege to compile and the response that I have received in this respect has again been overwhelming. The list of those individuals and organisations that have loaned photographs and provided information appears to be endless. In acknowledging their efforts in helping to make this book a possibility, I would sincerely like to thank: Mr Wyndam Angell, Mrs Mary Austin, Mr Howard Balston, Mr and Mrs John Blundell, Mr John Bridge, Mr (the late) and Mrs W.J. Cooper, Mr Ray Cottrell, Mrs Enid Crann, Mr Jason Crook, Mr John David, Mr Brent Davies, Mrs Janet Davies, Mrs Alison Dickinson, Mr Gareth Dowdell, Mrs Mary Edwards, Mrs Pam Freeman, Mrs Margaret Griffiths, Mr and Mrs Win Griffiths MP, Mrs Janet Hearle, Mr Clifford Hopkins, Mrs Anne Hunt, Mr and Mrs Tom Jones, Mr Paul Jones, Mr and Mrs Morgan Joseph, Revd Dr Graham, D. Loveluck, Councillor Mrs Madeleine Moon, Mr John Miskell, Miss Kathleen Munkley, Miss Millicent Munkley, Mrs Hilary Malvisi, Mr Ray W. Martin, Mr Peter Millis, Mrs Philip Missen, Mrs Gwyneth Osmar, Mr Gwyn Petty, Mr (the late) and Mrs Robert Proudfoot, Mr Fred H. Rees, Mr C.G. Reynolds, Revd Colin E. Richards, Ms Marilyn Richards, Mr Tom Sharpe, Mrs Sabrina Stoneman, Mr Gareth Thomas, Mrs Phyllis Endicott Thomas, Dr and Mrs Geoffrey G. Tinkler, Mr and Mrs David Trollope, Miss Millie Twist, Ms Rosemary Vaux, Mr John Williams (RNLI), Mrs Pam Williams, Mrs Jean Willment, Mrs L.M. Wilmot, Mr John Woods, Mr Tony Woolcott. Attwood & Sawyer Limited; Bridgend County Borough Council: Leisure Services Department; Grand Pavilion, Porthcawl; Porthcawl Tourist Information Centre; Library and Information Service, Bridgend and Porthcawl Libraries; *Glamorgan Gazette*; Glamorgan-Gwent Archaeological Trust; Kenfig Society; Madame Tussauds London; National Museum of Wales, Cardiff; Porthcawl Museum and Historical Society; Porthcawl Town Council; Ravenstone Public Relations Limited; Royal National Lifeboat Institution (RNLI), Porthcawl; Royal Porthcawl Golf Club.

I would like to thank the Bridgend and Porthcawl Libraries together with the Porthcawl Museum and Historical Society for allowing me free access to their archives for photographs and information. The ladies of both libraries deserve my appreciation for the help and assistance that they have given me in this respect. I am especially indebted to Mr Gwyn Petty for the many hours that he spent with me in the Porthcawl Museum selecting suitable photographs as well as for giving the book its final proof reading. Again, my gratitude to Mr Simon Eckley, my editor, for his guidance and advice in helping to bring the book to fruition. Finally, I would like to thank my wife Malvina for both her support and patience as well as for checking the contents and grammar of the book.

I regret if I have missed anyone in the above acknowledgements. If so, it has been entirely unintentional.

Foreword

By Win Griffiths MP (Bridgend)

Anyone who has read Keith's earlier book, *Around Kenfig Hill and Pyle*, will be delighted that he has spread his wings and given Porthcawl, Newton and Nottage the benefit of his enthusiasm and expertise. He has drawn together photographs illustrating virtually every aspect of the life of Porthcawl, Newton and Nottage, from the earliest times through the community's emergence as a thriving commercial centre and seaside resort to the present-day with all the necessary, and sometimes painful adjustments, that the decline of the coal industry and the changes in the holiday habits of people have brought about.

I am sure that the painstaking work that Keith and Malvina have done in putting together the photographs in this book will be well rewarded by the excitement and satisfaction of the readers as they find that long forgotten friend in a photograph – or even themselves – or recall a particular building or street scene now lost or dramatically changed.

The photographs range over the whole gamut of life in the story of the development of Porthcawl, Newton and Nottage. We are indebted to all those who contributed to this book by searching out their photographs – some of them no doubt long forgotten – but which now evoke past memories and bring the good, and perhaps not-so-good, times back to life again. Perhaps they will even confirm that the sun did shine more brightly in Porthcawl in our childhood and youth! I am sure that for me some of the photographs will revive happy memories of the Sunday school outings to Porthcawl over 40 years ago.

This book is a treasure trove for anyone wishing to steep themselves in their heritage, whether they have a personal interest in Porthcawl, Newton and Nottage, or a more general one in the story of South Wales over the years. I am thrilled to have been given the opportunity to write this foreword, and am confident that these photographs of Porthcawl, Newton and Nottage will entertain, excite, educate and illuminate the mind and memories of every reader.

Win Griffiths MP, outside the Palace of Westminster, London. Born in South Africa, he was educated at Brecon Boys' Grammar School and University College, Cardiff. He moved with his family to Cefn Cribwr in October 1980 and has been Bridgend's elected Labour representative in the Houses of Parliament since 1987. Prior to this and with an overlap of two years, Win was the Member of the European Parliament for South Wales from 1979 until 1989.

Introduction

I am very pleased that The History Press has again provided me with the opportunity to present a book in their *Archive Photographs* series. It has enabled me to bring together under one cover, and for the general enjoyment of everyone, some 220 photographs and prints of Porthcawl, Newton and Nottage. In addition to my own collection of photographs, I have been able to draw on those from the archives in the Bridgend and Porthcawl libraries, at the Porthcawl Museum and Historical Society and from many private collections. The photographs contained in the book cover a period from towards the end of the nineteenth century right up to the present time. A great number of these photographs have not been seen in public before.

Events and changes take place every day; this is history in the making. Photographs taken of these events and changes, as they happen, provide us with our archives for tomorrow. How thankful we are now for those opportunist individuals of the past, now often anonymous, who, sometimes only equipped with a Brownie box-camera, happened to be on the spot at the right time to capture that scene or special event for our delight and pleasure today. At the time, it might have seemed quite an unimportant occasion to the photographer. Maybe it was a casual family snap which just happened to have a significant building in the background, or a shot of an old vehicle such as a horse-drawn hearse, or perhaps a view of the countryside now obscured by building development, or a photograph taken on a day trip excursion on the train, of which all evidence of the railway line and its track now no longer exist. One could continue at length about all the different possibilities that photographs have of illustrating the everyday goings-on of the past.

In addition to the opportunist photographer, there were those forward-thinking individuals who actually went out with their cameras with the express intention of providing actual photographic records for the future. There have been many of these and I would like to think that I belong to this category. For many years, I have enjoyed the hobby of recording on film the changes that are taking place around us every day. Some of these are quite mundane and, more often than not, go by unobserved and unrecorded. When the changes are eventually noticed, it is often too late. What are familiar landmarks to us all such as bridges, shops, streets, even the local public transport bus, are with us one day and gone the next. And once gone, it is too late, the opportunity for taking photographs has also passed.

The photographs, that I have selected for inclusion in this publication, cover the changing life styles and habits in the community of Porthcawl, Newton and Nottage over many years.

As in my previous work, I have delved as far back as possible into the past to give the reader an insight into the full history of the area. Cameras were obviously not around in pre-historic or medieval times, but one can still capture on film the remains that have come down to us from those days of long ago. The dinosaurs, for example, even though they inhabited this area millions of years before man's emergence on the earth, left their footprints for us to record and display to everyone via the medium of photography. Photography, however, was only developed around the mid-1800s and since that time, we have a wealth of pictorial information to draw from.

Using examples of photographs, some taken before the turn of the century, together with illustrations, I have tried to chart the fortunes of the region from the past right up to modern times. These show the changes that have taken place in moving from a community basically dependent on agriculture, to one that went through both the growing pains and decline of the coal boom years as a busy and bustling port, before reaching its final emergence as an important seaside holiday resort. I have placed a special emphasis on the sea; it has always played an important role in the history of Porthcawl, Newton and Nottage. A both awesome and yet fascinating force, the power of the sea should never be under-estimated or taken for granted.

I very much hope that this book will provide pleasure and delight to all who acquire a copy. It will bring memories flooding back from the past, some of which, I have no doubt, will bear a tinge of sadness. I also trust that it will provide encouragement for readers to come forward with photographs for inclusion in future publications for this series.

Rough seas sweeping over the Esplanade in Porthcawl in the 1930s. At periods of high tide and when the weather was rough, the waves would regularly crash over the sea wall and promenade with the sea flooding into John Street and Mary Street.

One

Historical Background

A number of successive Ice Ages, together with the ebb and flow of the ocean tides over millions of years, have all failed to obliterate the footprints of Porthcawl's earliest inhabitants – the dinosaurs! The National Museum of Wales photograph shows the footprints of a three-toed dinosaur imprinted in a slab of pebbly sediment which was found covering a pool on the village green in front of Newton church in 1878. Altogether, five footprints have been preserved in the slab forming a distinctive track across its surface. Three of the prints were made by a left foot and the others by a right foot. The size and shape of these footprints, together with a length of about 0.5 metres for each single stride, suggest that they were made by a creature, albeit moving very slowly, about two metres tall that was able to walk fairly upright on its hind legs. The footprints, originally called *Brontozoum thomasi*, are attributed to a meat-eating two-footed dinosaur now reclassified as *Anchisauripus*. This dinosaur lived in the late Triassic Period about 215 million years ago. The name *thomasi* refers to T.H. Thomas, a wandering artist who originally found the specimen. The actual footprints were presented to the National Museum of Wales by Colonel Picton-Turbervill and are currently on display in the Museum at Cardiff. A plaster cast of the slab can also be viewed in Porthcawl Museum.

The Porthcawl area can be considered rich in terms of dinosaur evidence. The fossilised impressions of the jawbone and teeth of a flesh-eating dinosaur once called *Zanclodon*, but now referred to as *Megalosaurus*, were found at Stormy Down in 1898. In addition to those tracks found at Newton, the National Museum of Wales photograph above shows a cast of dinosaur footprints found at Nottage Court. The cast, with the footprints in relief, is in the collection of the Museum in Cardiff. The original slab has impressions made by two different reptiles: one track type is of *Anchisauripus* (the same as the Newton find), while the other is called *Otozoum* and may have been made by a relatively small, plant-eating dinosaur. All these dinosaur finds come from the late Triassic Period. In subsequent geological ages, Wales was gradually covered by the sea forcing the land-based dinosaurs to move on elsewhere to seek a more suitable habitat.

Archaeological evidence indicates that man had permanently settled in this area by the Neolithic Period (4500-2500 BC). In general, we only have knowledge of man's early existence from his burial sites, many of which have been found in and around Porthcawl, Newton and Nottage. The majority of these prehistoric burial mounds have now been examined or destroyed and levelled by building activities. Some mounds still exist, however, and can still be seen in the vicinity of Sker House and on Stormy Down. Probably the best example of these is that at Tythegston. Cae Tor is a small chambered cairn about 28 metres by 10 metres. The earth forming the mound has long been reduced in height, exposing the 4 metres by 2 metres single slab capstone of the burial chamber on which the author is seen sitting in the photograph. Other early remains have been found at Mount Pleasant on Newton Down where a Neolithic dwelling house was excavated in 1952 by the National Museum of Wales.

Various finds over the years have served to confirm man's long occupation of the area. Dan-y-Graig House, Newton, was the site of an archaeological excavation carried out by the Glamorgan-Gwent Archaeological Trust Ltd in 1985-86. The site of the dig was to the front of the sunken boundary wall in the foreground of the photograph. The present house was built in 1815 or soon after. In 1850, while new grounds were being laid out, a coin and other material of the Roman period were discovered.

A preliminary geological survey was carried out in November 1984 by the Mid Glamorgan County Council ahead of construction work to extend Dan-y-Graig House, which was by then an elderly person's respite home. This survey was observed by staff of the Glamorgan-Gwent Archaeological Trust who noted the presence of third century AD Romano-British coarseware. Following a small trial excavation in February 1985, two further larger scale planned excavations were undertaken in 1986. These involved the digging of the two exploratory trenches shown in the accompanying Glamorgan-Gwent Archaeological Trust photograph.

A number of Romano-British finds were uncovered as a result of the excavation undertaken by the Glamorgan-Gwent Archaeological Trust in the grounds of Dan-y-Graig House. These, together with the wall remains shown in the photograph, revealed that the site was part of a third-fourth century civilian complex. A subsequent geophysical survey of the area in April 1989 indicated the presence of a major Romano-British villa at Dan-y-Graig.

St David's Well, Ffynnon Dewi, Moor Lane, Nottage. The well, reputed to have been visited by St David during one of his pilgrimages in this area, gives its name to the ancient dell of Dewiscumbe (David's Valley) mentioned in the twelfth century grant of William, Earl of Gloucester to 'Richard de Cardiff of Novam Villam in Margan'. At some time in the past, there are indications that there was an inlet of the sea that encroached from the vicinity of Porthcawl point and extended past Nottage village. The original village, situated as it is on a small hillock, would have overlooked this inlet which possibly once reached as far as St David's Well. A small rivulet also discharged into the sea at this point. Eventually, the gradual formation over time of sand dunes on the foreshore, prevented the sea from entering the inlet. This action also caused the rivulet to form a lake known as The Rhyll just below the well. Subsequently, the water of both stream and lake sank through fissures and faults in the limestone rock to form an underground stream, leaving just a track through the dell where it had once flowed. Nowadays, this stream enters the sea via the outer harbour in the form of springs from under the old north dock. A number of farms in the Nottage area have taken advantage of the phenomenon of the underground stream by sinking artesian wells to pump up the water stored naturally below.

The Wilderness, Porthcawl, in the 1960s. Further downstream from The Rhyll and Nottage, the silting up of the old sea inlet resulted in the low-lying area becoming very marshy and liable to floods. The Wilderness has now lost its wild look. It has been drained and landscaped to form an attractive nature reserve and park.

The larger of the two ancient standing stones to be found on the edge of the Wilderness, Porthcawl. This stone stands about 140cm high and has a girth of 46cm at its widest point. Because of the shape of the stone, which has been attributed to the wear from ropes over many years, it is supposedly to have been used for the mooring of boats at the time when the Wilderness formed part of the inlet to the sea. Who can tell? The other standing stone is located nearby, but is of smaller size with less pronounced markings.

The village of Nottage is much older than either Newton or Porthcawl and dates back to the pre-Norman period. It has been suggested that, from earliest times, Nottage was built with defence strongly in mind. Using very low-draught boats, it would have been possible for both Viking and Irish pirates to have reached the village via any sea inlet which existed in the past. Old maps and ancient records indicate that there was both a chapel and graveyard in the village of Celtic origin. The stone being pointed out in the photograph above by Mrs Malvina Morgan, is in the wall surrounding the Village Green at Nottage. It is incised with a fleur-de-lis, thought to be part of an old tombstone from within the graveyard site located in the Green on the other side of the wall. The site of the chapel itself is off the photograph to the right of the Rose and Crown at Ashcott Villa. The Village Green was given to the community by the Nottage Court Estate in 1983.

Newton Village from the sand dunes in 1931. Once their 'Conquest' of England had been consolidated, the Normans turned their attention to Wales. By 1147, they had sufficiently advanced into south Wales for them to offer thanks for their victories by founding the Cistercian abbey at Margam. Some time after this date and before 1183, a grant of land, described as 'Novam Villam in Margan', was given to Richard de Cardiff. This was the beginning of Newton (New Town) village. The church of St John the Baptist, construction of which was started towards the end of the twelfth century and completed by 1189, bears the distinctive defensive features of the Norman period. As well as becoming a farming community, the natural haven at Newton enabled it to develop as a port of some repute over the next seven centuries. The 'Welsh Port Books, 1550-1603' attest to Newton's importance in this respect. For example, on 19 November 1601, two tons of iron as part cargo of *The Trynitye* of Aberthaw, were shipped from Newton to Minehead in Somerset.

St John's Well at Newton. This is situated to the south of the church and was originally called Sandford's Well after de Sanford, a Norman knight. In the Middle Ages, the well was supposed to possess both magical and holy properties. This attribute was due mainly to the fact that the well emptied itself when the tide came in and filled when the tide receded. It also had a reputation for curative properties right up to more recent times.

Ty Mawr or Nottage Court about 1885. Following the founding of Margam Abbey, Noge Court Grange as it was then called, was built by the monks to administer their agricultural land located in the Nottage area. Following the dissolution of the monasteries by King Henry VIII, the grange was bought in 1540 by Sir Rice Mansell. The Lougher family subsequently acquired the property five years later and rebuilt it in 1570 in the Elizabethan style; an 'E'-shape plan which remains to this day. It was known as Ty Mawr in 1846, but by 1877 the name had changed to Nottage Court. The white stone standing in front of the house is a Roman milestone which originally came from the Port Talbot area. Roman remains have, however, also been found in the grounds as well as the dinosaur footprints mentioned earlier. Note that the tramway track of the Duffryn Llynfi & Porthcawl Railway Company used to run directly past the right of the house.

Windmill remains on Newton Down. Except for the shipping activities from the small port at Newton, agriculture was the main occupation in the area. As there were no rivers or streams of any consequence in either Nottage or Newton suitable for powering watermills, at least two wind-driven mills were built in the locality.

The second windmill has been incorporated into Windmill House on South Road. This was called Windmill Cottage in 1884. The original curvature of the windmill shape is still apparent in the construction of the property on its left-hand side.

Two

Industry

James Brogden in a portrait taken from his own photograph album. Together with John his father, James is considered to be one of the fathers and pioneers of Porthcawl. Possibly the greatest influence on the expansion of Porthcawl was the Brogden family. They came from Sale, Manchester, and their arrival in the area about 1853 instigated the development of both local industry and the town of Porthcawl. The Brogden company – John Brogden & Sons – specialised in the mining of iron-ore and the construction of railways. It was this company that was instrumental in obtaining an Act of Parliament which was passed in 1864 to improve the Porthcawl Dock. Following his success in managing and developing the Tondu Ironworks, which the Brodgens had purchased when they first arrived in the area, James Brogden, the youngest of four sons and the junior partner in the company, was again chosen to be in charge of this major undertaking.

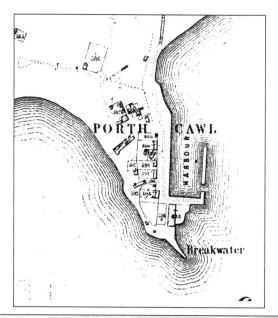

The extent of Porthcawl Dock in 1846. A group of local landowners and businessmen had obtained an Act of Parliament in 1825 to construct a jetty at 'Pwll Cawl' together with a tramroad linking that point with the Llynfi and Cefn areas in order to provide an outlet for the coal and iron industries. Porthcawl was chosen in preference to the small functioning port at Newton and a site at the mouth of the Ogmore River, both of which were considered unsuitable for the development. The tramroad of the Duffryn Llynfi & Porthcawl Railway Company was started in 1825 and at about the same time, a small tidal basin was constructed at 'Porth Cawl'. The latter basin was further extended northwards and coal loading facilities provided in 1840 by another Act of Parliament.

Porthcawl Docks and Railway together with the proposed new town as drawn up by the Brodgens about 1866. This plan formed the basis for the layout of Porthcawl as we know it today.

Work in progress on the extension of the main breakwater by a hundred yards and the construction of the lighthouse at Porthcawl, 1866. Frederick Appleby is seated in the centre of the group of three workmen. The white-painted lighthouse, which is made of cast iron, is a Grade II listed building. In 1911, the lantern was replaced following the loss of the original in a storm. Until it was converted to North Sea gas in 1974, the light was powered by town gas.

The opening ceremony of the New Porthcawl Dock on 22 July 1867. The new 547 ton SS (Screw Steamer) *John Brogden*, named after the head of the family partnership, John Brogden & Sons, led the vessels which entered the new dock as part of the ceremony.

Porthcawl Dock in the 1880s. The photograph shows the New Porthcawl Dock and inner dock gates, as opened in 1867. These two gates, each about 35-foot-wide, 40-foot-high and weighing many hundreds of tons, were manually controlled. A considerable amount of physical effort must have been required to operate the gates to enable sea water to be retained in the new 7.5 acre inner basin during low tide. The new dock was able to accommodate quite large vessels for those times. As a result, activity increased so much so that, by 1871, 165,000 tons of coal had been shipped from the dock. This was a big increase on the just over 17,000 tons recorded for 1864 before the development was started. Following a period of decline in the late

1870s, business again began to boom due to the expansion of the coal export trade. In 1889, the Porthcawl Dock handled more than 800 vessels accounting for a total of 227,000 tons. This, however, was Porthcawl's swan song as a port. Barry Docks were opened in July 1889 to be followed the next year by those at Port Talbot. As a direct result of the increased competition and the more sheltered situations offered by these new deep-water harbours, Porthcawl's trade rapidly dropped. By the year 1903, the dock was down to handling only 2,767 tons. The inner basin was closed three years later to be finally infilled in 1943 during the Second World War with waste from Ffordd-y-Gyfraith Colliery, Aberkenfig.

A general view of Porthcawl Dock about 1885 showing the inner basin with coal-loading hoists and chutes together with shipping. In those days, sail was still predominant although there were a number of steam-assisted vessels, including paddle-driven boats, which were gradually coming into use.

The *Nelson Hewerton* at Porthcawl Dock in 1877. Shipbuilding and repair work were carried out at Porthcawl over a number of years. The 1875 (first edition) 25-inch to the mile Ordnance Survey map of Porthcawl, clearly shows a shipbuilding yard and smithy at the north end of the dock's inner basin. Newspapers of the period also record the launching of a number of vessels from Porthcawl. This activity probably decreased dramatically when the inner basin was closed in 1906. However, it is recorded that between 1919 and 1925, at least eighteen ex-First World War ships were sold by the Admiralty to Messrs Hayes of Porthcawl for breaking up. These included thirteen destroyers, two paddle minesweepers, two coastal patrol vessels and an experimental steam submarine, HMS *Swordfish*. The latter was built in 1906 as a steam-driven prototype for a large class of ocean-going submarines. She was unsuccessful, however, because the steam condensed on the electrical switchgear causing explosions and she was converted to a surface patrol boat in 1918.

Development of Porthcawl Dock helped to spawn other small industries such as the Sibbering Jones Timber Yard shown here about 1892. This yard was located between the dock and the back of Railway Terrace (now Hillsboro Place). Albert Pearce, standing the other side of the saw blade, later went on to own the saw mill on Station Hill.

Gas Works and workers, Porthcawl, about 1920. The provision of public utilities went in step with the expansion and increase in prosperity of the town. The Porthcawl Gas, Light and Coke Company was formed and, by 1891, many parts of the town were illuminated by gas. The Gas Works was built on land adjacent to the present Griffin Park. Coal to make the coke and gas was transported to the works by wagons on a railway siding which ran from the dock along what is now the Eastern Promenade.

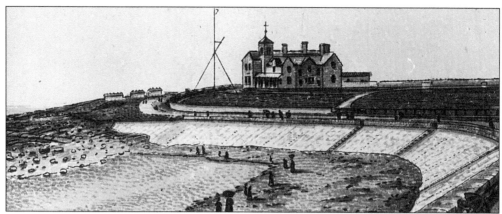

James Brogden's Esplanade, Porthcawl, about 1887. Following completion of work on the Porthcawl Dock and a period of absence from the area, James Brogden set about building his planned town, ably supported by his second wife Mary Caroline. He purchased an area of land in the region of Griffin Park and thirty acres on Pickets Lease. He employed two builders to carry out the work, George Dement and Joe Lill. John Street was the first road to be built and the first houses and shops were erected at the junction with Well Street. Work on the Brodgen residence, New House (later Sea Bank House and now the Seabank Hotel), was started about 1865. James Brogden also gave land for the National School in Lias Road and a plot on the corner of this road and John Street on which to build the Wesleyan chapel (now Trinity). The town continued to expand during the following years with a new railway station, a gas works and a shipbuilding yard being erected. The culmination of the Brogden's efforts, was the Esplanade which was completed in 1887. The latter had both a broad carriageway for vehicles and an equally broad promenade for pedestrians. The Esplanade Hotel was completed the same year to be followed in 1896 by the Marine Hotel.

The Brogden grave in Newton churchyard. The grave was refurbished and a new memorial stone befitting the part played by the Brogdens in Porthcawl's development, was erected in 1994 by the Porthcawl Town Council with the support of a number of organisations and individuals. The collapse of trade in Porthcawl's harbour from 1890 onwards had a disastrous effect on the fortunes of the Brogdens. James died in 1907, aged 75. His wife, Mary Caroline, was subsequently forced to sell Sea Bank House and other Brogden land. She resided for a time in the Esplanade Hotel before moving to 72 Victoria Avenue where she died at the age of 78 in 1927. The Brogdens are buried in line with the graves of the Knights, another distinguished family of the area, and close to the last resting place of Revd John Blackmore, the father of Richard Doddridge Blackmore, author of Lorna Doone and The Maid of Sker.

Lewis Place, Porthcawl, 1922. Development of Porthcawl continued along the lines drawn up by James Brogden. By the start of hostilities of the First World War, Suffolk Place, Westbourne Place, Victoria Road (now Avenue), George Street and Fenton Place were all built. Construction restarted again after the end of the war and the above photograph shows the members of the family of Mr T.W. Jones of 75 Suffolk Place involved in the building of Lewis Place. From left to right, back row: -?-, -?-, -?-, Norman Jones (son), Jim Jones (son), Billie Edwards (step-son), George Evans (nephew). Middle row: -?-, -?-, -?-, -?-, -?-, Charles Jones (son), Jack Whannel (son-in-law), Walt Hockings (?), Deeble (?).

Filling in part of the inner basin of Porthcawl Dock, 1913. The whole of the basin was finally and completely infilled in 1943.

In the wake of the decline of Porthcawl Docks, other 'replacement' industries began to grow. These mainly centred around the development of Porthcawl as a popular seaside and holiday resort which had started prior to the First World War. The amusement park at Coney Beach was opened on what had been the dock's ballast tip. Two ex-First World War aircraft hangars were erected on the site and the figure-8 ride, shown in the above photograph, was constructed in 1920-21. This ride, which became characteristic of the Coney Beach fun fair, had originally been used in a fairground at Oystermouth, Swansea.

Caravan and camping at Trecco Bay, Porthcawl, in the 1930s. At this time, the sand dunes are still present and the site is a long way from the order and size of its present layout. From records taken during the August Bank Holiday Week in 1945 and 1960, the numbers of campers and structures increased over this period of time from 10,936 and 1,706 to 16,257 and 3,273 respectively.

With the exception of the limestone quarries at South Cornelly, the days of heavy industry in the Porthcawl area have long gone. Porthcawl is now largely residential, catering in the main for the holiday trade. There are, however, some light industries in the area. Probably the most important and successful of these being Attwood & Sawyer, the manufacturers of Costume Jewellery. This firm was started in 1957 by Douglas Attwood (left of photograph), with his brother Horace (right) and Leonard Sawyer (centre).

The original business premises of Attwood & Sawyer was to the rear of the old co-operative store in John Street, Porthcawl; the whole area is now occupied by the John Street shopping precinct. With an expanding worldwide market for their costume jewellery, Attwood & Sawyer moved in 1964 to a new and more spacious modern factory in Woodland Avenue, Porthcawl.

These photographs show one of the well-appointed inspection rooms (above) and the polishing department (below) in the new Attwood & Sawyer premises. In January 1983, the company was bought out by Mr R.W. Martin, Mr P.J. Grourk and Mrs J.M. Davies. Since that time, business has greatly expanded. With a 200-strong workforce, everything from design to distribution is done from the Attwood & Sawyer base in Porthcawl. The company exports from here to more than sixty countries worldwide. The Attwood collection of costume jewellery is also sold on cruise ships, on international airlines, in duty free shops and in major departmental stores. It is also worn by many actresses on stage, screen and television, including the long-running American soap operas, *Dallas* and *Dynasty*. Attwood & Sawyer Ltd won the Best Costume Jewellery Award sponsored by Ballou Findings in 1993, the first year it was ever presented and completed a double by carrying off this sparkling accolade again in 1996.

Three

The Sea

High seas on the breakwater, Porthcawl. The sea has always made its presence felt at Porthcawl. The above view is characteristic of the rough seas often seen here during the period of high tides and when bad weather prevails. Gales whip up the waves so that they crash and break over the breakwater often obscuring the lighthouse at its end. In 1911, the conditions were so bad that the lantern on the top of the structure was washed clean away and had to be replaced. Before the beach in front of the Esplanade was surfaced to break up the waves, the sea also used to crash over the promenade and pour into both John Street and Mary Street under the same tidal and weather conditions. The sea around Porthcawl has always proved to be very treacherous for shipping as the many wrecks around the coast attest. The hidden rocks and sandbanks of Tusker, Sker and Scarweather, as well as those off Southerndown and Ogmore, have claimed their fair share of shipping over the years. The list of wrecks is long. Since the *Bona Ventura* foundered at Newton in 1694, there have been in the order of 120 recorded shipwrecks along the stretch of coastline between Nash Point and Kenfig Sands.

The grave of William Prout, aged 29, the captain of the *Olive Branch*, a fishing smack from Plymouth which was wrecked at Sker in December 1846. This memorial is to be found in the churchyard of St John the Baptist, Newton. All members of the three-man crew were lost. William Snowdon, aged 13, the mate from the same ship, is buried nearby. The churchyard is filled with many such graves bearing silent testimony to the souls of those drowned mariners and passengers from ships wrecked on these shores. Many are in unmarked graves and are scattered amongst the memorials to former residents of the area.

The wreck of the Bristol-registered sand dredger, *Steep Holm*, which grounded on Tusker Rocks, 3 October 1968. All the crew were saved thanks to the efforts of the Porthcawl Inshore Rescue boat and the Mumbles lifeboat. Three members of the Porthcawl crew – L.S. Knipe, J. Lock and R.A. Comley – were awarded framed letters of thanks from the chairman of the RNLI for their part in the rescue, while the coxswain of the Mumbles lifeboat, Lionel Derek Scott, won the Bronze Medal.

Wreck of SS *Samtampa* on Sker Rocks, April 1947. This was the worst ship wreck on Porthcawl coastline in living memory. Not only were all thirty-nine crew members of the *Samtampa* lost, but the eight-man crew of the Mumbles lifeboat were also all drowned when it capsized during rescue attempts. Bound for Newport where it was to undergo repairs, the former American Lend-Lease Liberty Ship was driven onto the rocks by 70 m.p.h. gales at 7 o'clock in the evening of Wednesday, 23 April 1947. Here, it broke into three pieces under the extreme ferocity of the wind and sea. Although the wreck was only 300 yards or so from the shore, rescuers were unable to do anything to help the marooned seamen who could be seen huddled together on the bridge of the ship. The winds were so strong that rockets carrying rescue lines were blown back on the would-be rescuers.

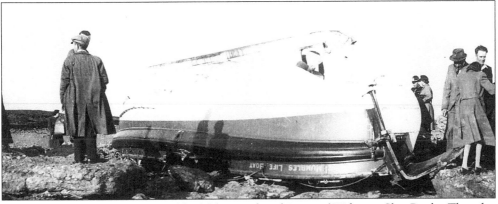

The remains of the wrecked Mumbles lifeboat, *Edward Prince of Wales*, on Sker Rocks, Thursday morning, 24 April 1947. Police and rescuers found the lifeboat, washed up and overturned about half a mile from the wreck of the *Samtampa*. The bodies of five of the lifeboatmen were found nearby. The Mumbles lifeboat had been launched on the Wednesday afternoon after an SOS had been received from the *Samtampa* reporting that she was in difficulties. After that, contact with the Mumbles lifeboat would have been very difficult. At the time of the disaster, it was not equipped with radio; communication was by lamps at night and semaphore by day. In paying tribute at the inquest, Mr B. Edward Howe, the Coroner for West Glamorgan, said, 'This was now another instance in which the Mumbles lifeboatmen had gone to the rescue of seamen in a storm of unexampled ferocity, so strong that in another part of the country the battleship *Warspite* was driven on the rocks and it was in a sea like that that the gallant men of Mumbles were ready to do their duty'.

Grave of some of the officers and crew of the SS *Samtampa* at Porthcawl cemetery. The memorial to the thirty-nine officers and crew who perished when the *Samtampa* was lost on Sker Rocks, was unveiled in the new cemetery at Nottage on Saturday, 23 April 1949, the second anniversary of the tragedy. The service was conducted by the Revd William Roach, Rector of Newton-Nottage, accompanied by the Revd Evan James and Mr Stanley Harvey, Port Missionary, Barry Dock, in the presence of Mrs Cynthia Lowe, widow of the Chief Officer of the *Samtampa* and other relatives and sympathisers. The bodies of the crew of the lifeboat, *Edward Prince of Wales*, were taken back to Mumbles and are buried in Oystermouth churchyard.

The memorial plaque to the SS *Samtampa* and the *Edward Prince of Wales* lifeboat, on Sker Rocks, near Porthcawl. This memorial, placed on the spot where the Mumbles lifeboat was found, was unveiled during a service of dedication held at Sker Point on Sunday, 26 April 1992. As a fitting start to the service, a lone maroon [firework] was sent snaking skyward as a solitary tribute to those thirty-nine mariners and eight lifeboatmen who perished on the cruel rocks on 23 April 1947. A specially invited congregation, numbering more than a hundred and including widows and relatives as well as members of the emergency services, attended the service of dedication. Father Jolyon Seward of Porthcawl conducted the service during which the 23rd Psalm and the traditional seamen's hymn, *Eternal Father, strong to save*, were sung. Throughout the service, the current Mumbles lifeboat and the Porthcawl Inshore Rescue boat, stood off Sker Point.

The Coastguards with their Board of Trade rescue appliance, outside the Rock Hotel, Porthcawl, about the time of the First World War. From left to right, the three coastguards are: Mr Proucc, Mr A. Smith and Mr Starkey. The civilians are: (second from left) Mr John David, coal merchant, and (fourth from left) Mr John Dare, baker. The Coastguards were founded in Porthcawl in 1834 and other than those associated with religion, it is the oldest organisation in the town. The first Coastguard station was built in the same year on the breakwater at Porthcawl, next to the round watch tower as shown in the photograph on page 36. The station was subsequently moved to other locations until 1965 when the present premises was built in Lock's Lane.

The Coastguards in action with their breeches boy equipment on Kenfig Sands on Sunday, 1 December 1946. The 10,448-ton American tanker, *Tillamook*, ran ashore off Sker Point, narrowly missing the rocks which were to prove so disastrous to the *Samtampa* the following year. The *Tillamook* remained aground on the sands until she was refloated some two months later. With the advantages subsequently offered by the RAF's helicopter service and the RNLI (Royal National Lifeboat Institution) Inshore Rescue boats for life saving and rescue work, the breeches boy equipment had been withdrawn from use by the Coastguards by 31 March 1988.

Signal station and pier, Porthcawl, 1900. The original Coastguard station is on the right of the photograph with the round watch tower and lighthouse to the centre of the view. The lighthouse supports its original lantern which was eventually blown away in the storm of 1911. Note the 'traffic lights' on the top of the round watch tower; these in their modern form, together with the tower, are still in everyday use today. The lights are not visible from the landward side, but are used by shipping to navigate into Porthcawl harbour.

The Coastguard look-out or watch tower on Lock's Common, Porthcawl, with Coastguard Officer Rixon and Landrover rescue vehicle, in the late 1970s. Mr Rixon served as a full-time officer from 1959 to 1979. The tower was brought into service on 15 April 1959 and was operated as a constant night watch station until *c.* 1984. It was dismantled in July 1986. The Coastguards in Porthcawl are on twenty-four-hour duty. The look-out tower, however, was only manned during the hours of darkness. There were never any lights provided in the tower so as to both ensure clear vision and also avoid the possibility of reflections in the glass windows which might have caused distress flares to be missed. The tower was eventually taken out of use because of improvements in communications with both radio and transport. Ship-to-shore radio and road vehicles were introduced in the 1960s. Regular vehicle watch patrols have been maintained along the coast ever since.

Prior to the formation of the Coastguards, surveillance along the coast was carried out by a 'Coast Waiter and Searcher'. Concerned with the number of shipwrecks and consequent loss of life that was occurring in the area, Mr Saunders of Newton, the Coast Waiter and Searcher at that time, wrote to both the Revd Robert Knight, Newton, and Colonel Knight, Tythegston, on 28 August 1815. His was a plea for a life saving boat to work up to four or five miles off-shore from Porthcawl. Following recent wrecks, the cause was taken up by the reverend gentleman who opened a fund in 1821 to purchase such a lifeboat, but nothing ensued. It took another disaster on 23 October 1859, when a boat was lost with all hands, to resurrect the matter. The RNLI Inspector recommended the purchase of a suitable craft and on 29 April 1860, the six-oared *Good Deliverance* lifeboat was inaugurated. This craft saw service from 1860 until 1872 to be followed by the *Chafyn Grove* (1872-87) and the *Speedwell* (1887-1902). This etching of the launching of the lifeboat at Porthcawl, also shows the bridge over the slipway. The bridge, which restricted launching at high water, was constructed in 1879 by the Dock Company.

The first lifeboat house, adjoining No 12 Marine Terrace on the Esplanade at Porthcawl, was built on ground kindly given by Lady Windsor and was completed in April 1860 at a cost of £120. The above view, taken at the beginning of this century, clearly shows the house protruding out onto the promenade where it can still be seen to this day. In 1872, it was enlarged to accommodate the larger *Chafyn Grove* lifeboat. The Porthcawl lifeboat station was closed in 1902 and the following year the old lifeboat house was sold for £160. The premises is now occupied by an Indian take-away.

37

The *Speedwell* lifeboat at Porthcawl. This picture of a procession, in which the *Speedwell* and its team of launching horses took part, together with members of the Foresters and Oddfellows clubs, would have been taken sometime between 29 September 1887 and 1902 when this boat saw service at Porthcawl. Like its predecessor, the *Chafyn Grove*, the *Speedwell* was a 34 feet by 8 feet self-righting vessel, built by Forrest & Sons. It was equipped with ten oars, carried a crew of thirteen and had cost £480 to construct when given to the RNLI by Miss Jane Houghton of London.

Mr and Mrs James Pearce, *c.* 1857. Pilot James Pearce of Porthcawl, together with fellow pilots, John Jones and Thomas Pearce and Seaman George Clark, each won the RNLI Silver Medal and a sum of money by helping to save three out of four men on board a wrecked ship on 29 March 1857. The vessel in question, was the schooner, *Trevaunance*, out of St Ives, Cornwall, which struck a sandbank off Porthcawl. The stranded men had taken to the rigging of the vessel and James Pearce volunteered, with his colleagues, to try and get them off. This they succeeded in doing after many hours and with great danger to themselves. After spending sixteen hours in the rigging, three of the unfortunate crew members were saved; the fourth man was missing and his body was not recovered. Alas, Thomas Pearce himself became a victim of the sea and was drowned the following year on 26 August 1958 in the duty of his calling.

Tea pot and stand depicting the *Speedwell* lifeboat and Porthcawl Docks. This example of imported china-ware dates from around the turn of the century and was typical of the type of embossed souvenir of the period visitors would take home as a 'Present from Porthcawl'. Some things never change!

Mr Albert Pearce (of Park Avenue), last of Porthcawl's early lifeboatmen; the end of an era came with his death, at the age of 87, in April 1970 and a family sea-faring tradition was interrupted. His great-uncle, Juniper Pearce, was connected with Porthcawl's first two lifeboats, the *Good Deliverance* and the *Chafyn Grove*, in about 1860. James Pearce, another relative, was second coxswain of the *Speedwell* lifeboat from 1877 to 1881, when he was appointed coxswain, a post he held until 1902 when the Porthcawl lifeboat station closed. Albert Pearce began his career in lifeboats as a young lad in 1899 and his brother, Fred, was the last of the Porthcawl pilots. In 1928, Albert received a letter of thanks from Porthcawl Council praising his bravery and heroism in saving the lives of five sailors from the SS *Kendy* which had capsized a quarter of a mile off Porthcawl seafront. He was also one of the founder members of Ye Olde Pirates Club.

Launching Inshore Rescue lifeboat No. 52 on the slipway at Porthcawl harbour, *c.* 1965. This was the first craft to be based at the new RNLI Inshore Rescue boat station which was established at Porthcawl in May 1965. A temporary lean-to shelter on the side of Jennings Warehouse was leased from the Porthcawl Urban District Council. The inflatable rescue boat was the first lifeboat to return on a permanent basis to Porthcawl since the *Speedwell* was withdrawn in 1902. The clock has tuned a full circle, however, with the new inshore craft using the very same slipway alongside the breakwater as its predecessors.

RNLI Inshore Rescue lifeboat D. 174 in action off Porthcawl, *c.* 1968.

During the Second World War, RAF Air Sea Rescue launches were based at Porthcawl and moored in the outer harbour. As well as rescuing many servicemen, the RAF boats and crew were also instrumental in the saving of both sailors and civilians that got into difficulties in the sea off Porthcawl. The RAF Marine Unit remained at Porthcawl until well after the end of hostilities. The colours were finally lowered on 23 February 1959 and the RAF launches sailed away.

Developed during the Second World War, the Sea King helicopter has subsequently proved its worth with the RAF Air Sea Rescue Unit in successfully carrying out rescue work time and time again. This one is shown during an exercise off the pier at Porthcawl in the late 1980s.

Porthcawl Life Saving Rescue Team and Coastguards, 1936.

The Duke of Kent, who was on a helicopter tour of RNLI installations, inspects the Inshore Rescue lifeboat during his visit to the Porthcawl RNLI station on 1 November 1979. Porthcawl has now received its latest craft, an Atlantic 75 rigid inflatable inshore lifeboat. This boat is 7.3 metres long and, with a crew of three, can attain speeds of 32-34 knots. The new RNLI lifeboat station at Porthcawl, built to house this rescue craft together with its launching Talus-MBH tractor and DoDo cradle, was officially opened on 7 September 1996.

Four

Commerce and Trade

Frank's General Provisions shop in John Street, Porthcawl, in the early 1900s. The store, also proud to show that Frank's had branches at Cardiff and Ilfracombe, formed part of the frontage of the Coliseum cinema. The windows and balcony of the old picture house are shown to the top of the photograph and can still be seen on the building today. The balcony was used to declare local government election results.

Looking north up John Street, Porthcawl, in the early days of this century. The old post office is on the left of picture on the corner of John Street and Well Street – the site now occupied by Sidoli's Ice Cream Parlour. The post office, built about 1871, also served as the telegraph office. James Pearce's Commerce House was on the other corner. The Porthcawl Hotel, which was built in 1884 and extensively enlarged just before 1891, stands on the opposite side of the road and is still recognisable today.

Dare's Restaurant, John Street, Porthcawl, about 1910. The restaurant was situated on the opposite side of John Street facing the Porthcawl Hotel.

J. House & Sons, the Standard Bakery in John Street, Porthcawl, early 1900s.

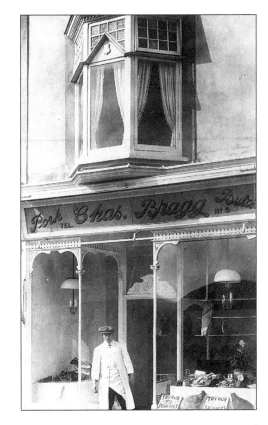

Charles Bragg, pork butcher, New Road, Porthcawl, c. 1910.

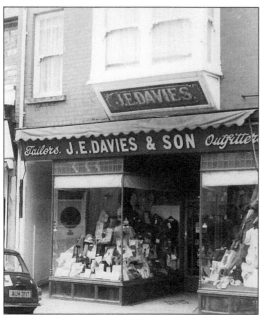

J.E. Davies, Cloth Hall – Gents' Outfitters, John Street, Porthcawl. The beautifully maintained, stained wood frontage looks the same today as it did when installed at a cost of £1,000 in 1936. This was an enormous sum in those days, but look what you get when you pay for quality! J.E. Davies' has been in the same family for over eighty years – the longest period of continuous family ownership for any of the shops in the town. The sign below the bay window has been there since the shop first opened.

The Speedy Shoe Repairs, South Road, Porthcawl, 9 January 1988. This is a traditional cobbler's shop which was run for many years by the late Mr Edward Loveluck. The business is now owned by Mr John Miskell who is shown standing outside his lock-up shop. Mr Miskell still uses cobbler's skills from the past, such as iron shoe lasts, when repairing footwear. At one time, everyone used to have their shoes repaired. It was all hobnails, studs and patches. There was no rubber used. Complete bends of tanned leather were delivered to the shop and heels and soles were cut from them to fit each individual shoe for repair. However, rubber-soled shoes guaranteed for six months and the advent of new high bonding glues introduced in the 1960s, brought about a revolution in the manufacture of footwear and the craft of cobbling. Nevertheless, trade is still brisk at Speedy Shoe Repairs.

Angell's the butcher, Nottage village, 23 November 1991. Previously run for many years by Mr Tantum, the shop was taken over in 1991 by Mr Wyndham Angell. The premises date back to the sixteenth century and occupies what was once the stables of West End Farm. The shop-front is on the side of the building in what was the old farm yard and pound.

The village shop, Nottage village square, c. 1933. From left to right, standing in the shop doorway: F.H. Rees, Walter Bell (the shop proprietor), Emily Gillert, Florence Street, Charlie Morgan (Ashcott Villa).

Comley's grocer's shop, New Road, 1949. From left to right: Elizabeth Brown, Donald Comley, Betty James.

Get your *South Wales Echo* here. R. Longman, newsagent and confectioner, The Huts, Newton, *c*. 1920. From left to right: George Farr (1895-1972) and Daisy Longman.

J. House & Sons, New Road, Porthcawl, *c.* 1910. On the horse-drawn delivery van, which was typical of the period, the firm proudly states 'J. House & Sons. The Standard Bakery. Families Waited Upon Daily. Agents for Lipton's Teas'.

'Jones the Milk' with his Austin delivery van in Meadow Lane, Porthcawl, 1955.

The Seabank Hotel, Porthcawl, commanding a fine view out over the Bristol Channel, from a postcard franked in 1920. Originally built about 1865 as New House, it became Sea Bank House, the private residence for many years of Mary Caroline and James Brogden. As early as 1892, with the Revd E.J. Newell as its principal, it became Porthcawl College for Boy Boarders. Following James Brogden's death in 1907, the year after Porthcawl ceased operating as a coal exporting port, Mary Charlotte was forced to sell the house to a Mr John Elias and others. Subsequently, the property was developed commercially to become the Seabank Hydro and then the Seabank Hotel.

The Esplanade and Marine hotels, Porthcawl, late 1920s. Like the Seabank Hotel, these two hotels are situated in a prime position on the sea-front. The Marine Hotel and Marine Terrace were built in 1886 and the following year, the Esplanade and the Esplanade Hotel were completed. The Esplanade Hotel was designed in such a manner that if it failed as an hotel, it could be converted into dwelling houses.

Five

Transport

Pine's Airways poster, 1936-39. What a pleasure and a treat it would be, to fly at these prices today!

George Stanley Pine in his flying kit, 1938. He came from a local family that had a long history in the transport business, especially in the hire of carriages for weddings and funerals. George flew his first plane, a Gipsy Fox Moth, on 15 April 1936, on a flight from Gravesend to Porthcawl. The aerodrome, where he established his Pine's Airways, was in a field on the corner of Lock's Lane and the Common. From here, he gave passengers trips over Porthcawl, the Bristol Channel and the surrounding countryside. The business ceased on the outbreak of the Second World War when he joined the Air Transport Auxiliary and served in the Far East for three years.

Pine's Airways Gypsy Fox Moth at a Whitchurch garden party, pre-Second World War. The pilot, George Pine, can be seen sitting in the open cockpit of the aeroplane. The two passengers sat up-front and inside the fuselage, one behind the other, and protected from the elements by windows. Right behind the engine, it would be a noisy ride by today's standards!

Putting Porthcawl on the map! Having had an airline of the status of Imperial Airways landing at the Flying Field on Lock's Common, Porthcawl can truly say it has been served by land, sea and air transport. The photograph shows the famous British aviator, Sir Alan John Cobham, with local councillors on his arrival at Porthcawl in 1932 with a flight of twelve aeroplanes. He was welcomed by the Chairman of Porthcawl Council, Cllr Russell Mabley JP, and lunched in the Esplanade Hotel. Friday, 3 June 1932 was to be Aviation Day for Porthcawl with Sir Alan presenting Britain's greatest air display at the Flying Ground. Flying was from 11.30 a.m. with a programme covering twenty events. These included 'unique aerobatic displays', upside-down flying, aeroplane-towed gliding, a thrilling pylon race, parachute descents, passenger flights in three-engined airliners, wireless controlled flying and the autogiro. Altogether, twelve aircraft took part and The Golden Arrow, Sir Henry Segrave's racing car, was on view throughout the day. Admission was 1/3 for Adults and 6d for Children. Car Parking 1/- and Flights were from 4/-. The show was a great success with thousands of spectators visiting the Flying Ground. Sir Alan, the organiser of the event, after serving with the RAF during the First World War, entered the field of civil aviation and became one of its trail-blazers. The aeroplane, pictured above, was one of two entirely new British three-engined biplanes, described as the most interesting on show at the air display. Many took the opportunity to fly in the three-engined Airspeed airliner.

Bow wagon at Ty Coch Farm, Porthcawl, 1920s. This was the traditional form of farm transport that had been used for generations. It was also used for carnival events in very much the same way as lorries are today.

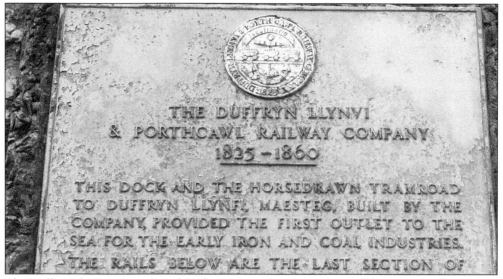

The Duffryn Llynfi and Porthcawl Railway Company was inaugurated by an Act of Parliament which received the Royal Assent on 10 June 1825. By this Act, a tramway was run from the Duffryn Llynfi to 'Porth Cawl' for the purpose of transporting coal and iron to a new dock to be built at this point. Work commenced in 1825 and the tramway was opened for horse-drawn traffic in 1828. In 1846, the Llynfi Valley Railway was incorporated and the following year took over the Duffryn Llynfi and Porthcawl Railway Company. With the increase in trade to the Porthcawl Dock, it became necessary to convert the tramway to steam traction and in 1861, broad-gauge rails replaced the old tramway from Tondu to Porthcawl. On 1 August 1865, the broad-gauge track was in its turn replaced by standard gauge and Porthcawl Dock became the locomotive terminus for locomotive railways from both the Llynfi and Ogmore valleys. At the time of its demise in 1861, horse-drawn trams were making five daily six-hour through journeys in each direction on the old tramroad between Tondu and Porthcawl. Nottage House was the tramway superintendent's house; the garage that housed his own personal railway carriage can still be seen on the north approach to the property. The original bridge that carried the tramroad over Moor Lane is also still intact. Jennings Warehouse on the harbour, now a Grade II listed building, was built in 1832 as an iron warehouse and is the only one in the town that was associated with the Duffryn, Llynfi and Porthcawl Railway. It is the oldest 'maritime' building in Wales. A short stretch of tramway is preserved on the breakwater near the Jennings building. This is surmounted by the memorial plaque shown above.

Porthcawl's first railway station, South Road, at the turn of the century. This station, which was at the top of Station Hill, was opened in 1876 and remained in use until 1916 when the new station was built. The first station-master was Mr Charles Dalby. The picture views the station looking north with South Road on the left. New Inn in the centre, has now become the Sea Horse. The boundary wall between the station and South Road still exists and contains many examples of the characteristic two-hole tramway sleeper stones of the old Duffryn, Llynfi & Porthcawl Railway.

The staff of the original Porthcawl railway station, South Road, at the turn of the century.

The new station at Porthcawl when it opened in 1916. The station and railway line survived until 1964 when they were both removed under the Beeching axe. The railway track was taken up and eventually the new Portway road was laid over the route.

The staff at Porthcawl's new station in 1916.

The original route of the Duffryn, Llynfi and Porthcawl Railway, ran right alongside and very close to Nottage Court. When steam locomotives were introduced in 1861, the original route of the track passed unacceptably close to this property and a tunnel was therefore constructed under the village of Nottage. It started to the north of Ty Talbot farm, and finished just south of Nottage Forge before Windmill House.

George Howell and chum, on a shunter at Porthcawl, *c.* 1955.

Paddle steamers plying their trade at the breakwater, Porthcawl, turn of the century. Sea trips were very popular at this time with steamers calling at many of the ports and seaside resorts on both sides of the Bristol Channel.

The coming of motorised road transport saw a big increase in the number of day trippers and sightseers to Porthcawl. The photograph illustrates this trend and shows both charabancs and motor cars on the Esplanade in the early 1930s.

Railway pannier tank engine on the triangle track with day trip coaches parked on the old Salt Lake behind, late 1950s.

Every town seemed to have its railway level crossing with its inevitable delays to both vehicular and pedestrian traffic when the gates were closed to allow a train to pass through. Porthcawl was no exception to this rule. This was the scene at the top of Station Hill in the early 1950s just after such a delay when the gates had at long last been re-opened. The problem was removed once and for all when the Beeching axe fell on the Porthcawl branch railway line in 1964.

The scene at Rest Bay, Porthcawl, not long after the end of the Second World War. Many cars had been off the road and up on jacks for the duration of the war due to the petrol rationing. With demobilisation behind them, now was the time for servicemen and their families to get out and about on the roads again.

Six

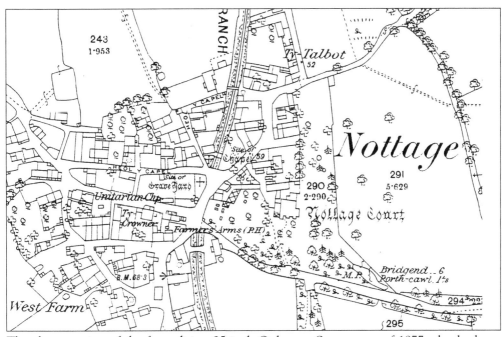

The above section of the first edition 25-inch Ordnance Survey map of 1877, clearly shows the sites of both chapel and graveyard in Nottage village. Ashcott Villa, next to the Rose and Crown, now stands on the ground originally occupied by the chapel. The site of the graveyard is on the Village Green where human skeletal remains were unearthed at the eastern end during construction work on the tunnel for the Porthcawl branch railway line. The tunnel runs directly below the village at his point as can be seen from the map. The photograph on page 16 shows the inscribed stone that can be seen in the boundary wall of the green. It is a fleur-de-lis and possibly comes from one of the gravestones in the original burial ground. There is no doubt that a chapel once existed in Nottage as there are many references to it in ancient manorial and other records. It may have been an early Celtic cell associated with St David's Well or perhaps a church belonging to the Noge Court Grange that was used by the monks as their place of worship.

St John the Baptist church, Newton, prior to 1903 when the lych gate was erected in memory of the late Revd Richard Wake Gordon. The building of the church is thought to have been started some time towards the end of the twelfth century and was completed by 1189 when the first Rector was installed. It was designed around the massive embattled tower as a place of defence as well as one of worship. Subsequent to that period, the structure has been altered and refurbished over the centuries (most notably between 1485 and 1495 by Jasper Tudor), but the church still retains its basic and distinctive early Norman characteristics.

The pulpit in St John the Baptist's church, Newton, at the beginning of this century. The pulpit is of pre-Reformation origin and is very rare, if not unique. In 1826-27, the Rector, the Revd Robert Knight carried out extensive alterations to the church, including those to the pulpit. Prior to this time, the pulpit had protruded by about five feet into the nave. The arch above the pulpit is decorated with two angels framing their heads with their wings while the semi-circular stone pulpit itself bears carvings which depict the flagellation of Jesus. Christ is shown clean shaven which is unusual.

The interior of St John the Baptist church, Newton, early 1900s. The stone pulpit can be clearly seen on the left of the photograph.

Summer fête at St John the Baptist church, Newton, 1982. From left to right, standing: Arabella Davies, Helen John, Juliet Anthony, Rebecca Stockdale, Rachel Stockdale, Sally Anthony. Kneeling: Caroline Bell, Zoe Burrows.

Hope Chapel on Newton-Nottage Road, Porthcawl, 1931. About 1808, the Independents were holding services in a house in Newton called Bethel with their first minister being William Williams. Steps were taken to build a permanent chapel and this came to fruition in 1828 when Hope Independent Chapel was opened. By 1890, it had a congregation of seventy-eight.

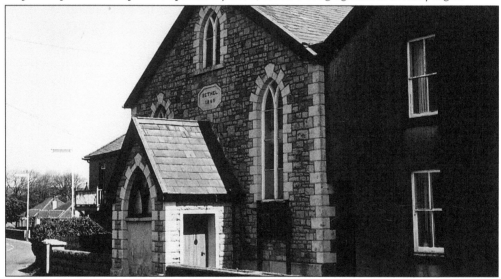

Bethel Chapel, South Road, Porthcawl. The Calvinistic Methodist Chapel celebrated its hundredth anniversary on 16 May 1965. Prior to being built in 1865, a few Calvinistic Methodists had held a Sunday school in the loft of the Victoria public house as early as 1859. Not long after this time, George Sibbering, a timber merchant of Merthyr Tydfil bought Windmill House and surrounding land in South Road and came to live in Porthcawl. The Sibberings were Independents, but nevertheless Mrs Mary Sibbering offered a piece of land to the Methodists so that they could build a place of worship in the parish. After many meetings of the Methodist churches in the locality, it was eventually agreed to accept the offer and building work commenced in 1864. Before its completion, however, it was decided that a larger structure would be needed for a chapel and more land was obtained on lease. The original building became the chapel house and Bethel Chapel itself was completed and opened on 29 and 30 May 1886 and not 1885 as shown on the building.

Looking north from what is now John Street, c. 1880. The Wesleyan Chapel, which is on the right, was built on land at the corner of John Street and Lias Road given by James Brogden and opened in 1871. The Wesleyans' first meeting place was near the docks and it is recorded that an inspector made a call on the Sunday school there in 1842. The chapel was subsequently amalgamated with Highfield United Reformed Church in 1984 to form what is now Trinity Church. The Revd Colin E. Richards was appointed the first minister of the combined congregations. The National School, Lias Road, can be seen on the left of the photograph. The school, which was often mistaken as a church because of its bell tower, was built in 1873. However, until 1914 when the new All Saints' Church was consecrated, services had been held in the school rooms. Philadelphia Road, construction of which began about 1847, can be distinguished in the background while the early houses of Victoria Road (later Avenue), are prominent in the centre. Miss Howell's High School for Girls (now David & Snape, solicitors) is next to the Wesleyan Chapel.

The Highfield United Reformed Church in Highfield Avenue, Porthcawl, prior to its demolition in 1984. Highfield Church, itself, had been built in 1872.

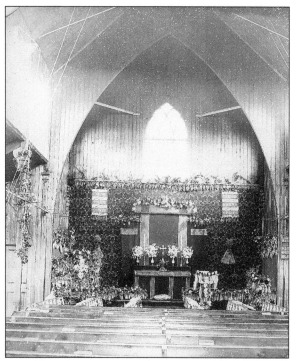

The interior of All Saints' Church, Porthcawl, at the beginning of the century. By 1891, the population of Porthcawl had grown to nearly 1,000 and the building of a new church was considered a necessity. Ground on which to build the proposed new church was given by Lord Wimborne. This acre of land was on the corner of Victoria Road (now Avenue) and the north end of Mary Street which later became Church Place. An estimated costing of £4,000 had been obtained for building a permanent church, but instead a corrugated iron church was erected in its place. This was opened on 1 November 1892, All Saints' Day, and it served the parish until the spring of 1914 when the present church opened its doors. The original church was dismantled and taken to Maesteg where it was re-erected as a mission church.

The clergy and choir of All Saints' Church, Porthcawl, possibly following the consecration service held by the Bishop of Llandaff in the spring of 1914. Robed members, from left to right, back row: -?-, Mr Deere, Mr Billy Oliver (fruiterer, John Street). Second row: -?-, -?-, -?-, -?-, -?-, Mr Bagg, Mr C. Williams (coal merchant), Mr King, -?-, Mr Cyril John, -?-, Mr Bragg, Mr W.H. Brown. Front row: -?-, -?-, Mr Fred Brown, Revd T. Holmes Morgan, Rector of Newton-Nottage, Revd Hector Evans. Mr Elward Deere is standing on the left of the group. The Foundation Stone behind the choir states: 'A.M.D.G. This stone was laid by George Edward Blundell Aug 7th. 1912.' The church building, less porches, side chapel, vestry and tower, and costing approximately £9,750, was consecrated by the Bishop of Llandaff on Wednesday, 11 February 1914. The porch, lady chapel and vestry were added in 1964-65. The planned tower is still conspicuous by its absence and the exposed brickwork on the south-facing wall of the church can still be seen today.

Civic Sunday, Porthcawl, 1935.

Noddfa, Capel y Bedyddwyr, Philadelphia Road, Porthcawl. The Welsh Baptist cause was re-established in Porthcawl in 1937 by the late Revd T. Thomas of Arlington Place. The first service was held in the Girl Guides' Hall on Sunday, 24 January 1937 and conducted by the Revd Thomas. In due course, land was purchased in Philadelphia Road and the building of the chapel commenced in 1939. The chapel, costing nearly £5,000, was completed despite the outbreak of the Second World War and opened on Sunday, 7 August 1940. It was the only church in the United Kingdom to be granted this dispensation because of wartime building restrictions.

St David's Church, Nottage, prior to its demolition in January 1992. Not long after the end of the Second World War, the Rector of Newton-Nottage, the Revd (later Canon) William Roach, took steps to have a church built in Nottage. This small wooden church was erected in 1948 on land kindly given by Mr J.K. Blundell. The building was an ex-Church Army hut that had been purchased from a RAF camp. The site had been used by the American forces during the war and two buildings that they had left were also acquired. These were used as a school room and anteroom. The small mission church was dedicated to St David and consecrated by the Bishop of Llandaff on 24 March 1948.

The new St David's Church at Nottage under construction in 1992. To cater for the growing community at Nottage, it was decided to build a new church on the existing site. This meant that the existing wooden church would first have to be demolished to make way for the new. Sufficient funds were raised through public subscriptions and donations and it was decided to start work in January 1992 with Mr Peter Millis of Nottage as architect. Following the completion of the 1991 Christmas religious festival, the momentous occasion arrived and work started at the beginning of January 1992 on the demolition of the old church. This was a sad time for many, but the bell was saved and has been re-hung for use in the new church. The new St David's Church was consecrated on 15 November 1992.

Seven

Education

A young and demure Millie Twist at Moorlands School, New Road, in the early 1920s. Millie had previously attended Miss Howell's High School for Girls in Lias Road. This was a private preparatory school opposite the National School in the building which is now occupied by David & Snape, solicitors. Even though Miss Howell took in boarders, Millie attended the school as a day scholar, travelling daily by train from Kenfig Hill. She studied with Miss Howell for 18 months before enrolling at Moorlands as a boarder. Here Millie found study more rewarding and stayed for seven happy years until she left at the age of sixteen. Meanwhile, in 1929, Miss Howell went on to build the Porthcawl College for Girls in Lougher Gardens, and it is interesting to note that old girls of both her schools still hold an annual reunion.

Education can be said to have started in the area in 1738 when two circulating charity schools were established, one in Nottage and the other in Newton. Griffith Jones (1683-1771) of Llanddowror in the Teifi Valley was the dynamo behind this scheme to establish temporary schools in areas throughout Wales, usually in the winter months, which concentrated on teaching children and adults to read their mother tongue. The explicit intent of this was to strengthen the hold of the Christian religion amongst the masses through giving them personal access to the Bible and by 1771, it has been estimated that over two hundred thousand people, almost half the population of Wales had attended these schools. They were followed by the creation of permanent once-a-week Sunday schools and eventually by single-teacher establishments often known as 'Dame schools'. Such places of education were usually held in private residences and run by either an elderly man or woman who possessed a basic knowledge of teaching. Typical of such a school was the Porthcawl Academy although the exact location of this school is not known. From this report written by Mr Samuel Price on 19 September 1873, concerning the progress of one Master John Rodrick, we can perhaps discern that obedience and docility were qualities demanded of pupils there.

> Porthcawl Academy
> Sep. 19th 1873.
>
> Dear Sir –
>   I am most happy to inform you, that Master John, your son has made a considerable progress with his lessons, during the last quarter. He has proved himself both obedient and docile.
>
>   I am, Dear Sir,
>   Your respectfully
>   Samuel Price.
>
> Mr D. Rodrick.

A typical classroom setting in Moorlands School during the 1930s. Note the pew-style desks which were characteristic of most schools until development took place following the end of the Second World War.

Opposite: Moorlands School was a boarding and day school for girls which survived until the Second World War. It was situated in a building which still exists at the Newton end of New Road. The principals of the school were the Misses Garsed. Prior to starting at Moorlands, these two ladies had run a preparatory school for young boys, first in John Street and then in Gordon Road.

The National School, Lias Road, Porthcawl, being demolished in April 1962. Following the Elementary Education Act of 1870, and on the instigation of the Rector, the Revd E.D. Knight, this National School was built in 1873. The new school's first headmaster was Mr William Rees.

The National School's hockey team about 1908. In the back row, fourth and fifth from the left, are Cissie House and Queenie Griffin, while Margaret Matthews (*née* Thomas) is second from the left in the middle row.

The staff and students of Porthcawl College, 1896. The principal, the Revd E.J. Newell MA, in mortar-board and gown, is in the centre of the group with Mr J. Towns on his right. Note the trellis-style façade which can be clearly identified as that of Sea Bank House on early photographs of this period.

Staff and pupils of St John's School, Newton, about 1923.

St David's Day celebrations at New Road School, Porthcawl, 1928. Morgan Joseph is on the left with the sword and large shield. The headmaster at this time was Mr J. Baker.

Headmaster, Mr Leonard S. Higgins OBE, MA, with the prefects of Porthcawl Secondary School about 1935. Mr Higgins was the author of the authoritative book on the history of the area entitled *Newton Nottage and Porthcawl (From Prehistoric Times to 1950)*.

Newton Junior School, St David's Day, 1976.

West Park Primary School, Nottage – the winning team in the Urdd Eisteddfod, 1978.
Mr Haydn David MA, the headmaster, is seated second from the left in the front row.

Cardiff Camp School, c. 1945. From left to right, front row: Miss Watt, youth organiser; Mr Walter Maidment, Centre Youth Club; Miss Watts, pianist. Back row: school kitchen and garden staff standing in between Sister Elsie, Jerusalem church (first on the left) and Mrs L.M. Wilmot, Girls Guildry leader, Splott Baptist Church, Cardiff (first on the right). The chef was known as 'Cookie' to all who attended the school. He was famous for his buns that were had with tea once a week. These were 'home-made' in the school kitchen. When it started life in 1936, it was known as the Cardiff City School Camp. At the time of its closure and subsequent demolition in 1994, it was called the Outdoor Studies Centre. Up to the time of its Golden Jubilee celebrations in 1986, well over a quarter of a million children had attended the school. These had included Miss Shirley Bassey who, when she attended courses at the school as a junior pupil, used to entertain the others by dancing and singing on the stage in the dining room.

Cardiff Camp School, 1945-6. Parents' day for the Girls Guildry, Splott Baptist Church, Cardiff. Mrs & Revd Rodd are seated centre with Mrs L.M. Wilmot, Guildry leader, standing behind and between them.

Eight

Organisations

Policemen stationed at Porthcawl before the First World War. From left to right, back row: PC D. Grant, PC W. Thomas, PC Hayes. Front row: PC William Richardson, station sergeant; PC F. Trott. PC William Richardson gave the following account of his experiences: 'With the exception of the Sergeant, myself and the other four boys volunteered for the Welsh Guards on their formation in May 1915. The battalion (including ourselves), left for France in Aug 1915. PC Grant was killed on the first day of action at Loos. PC W. Thomas died after having had both feet amputated. PC F. Trott died of wounds on the day Armistice was signed, 11 Nov 1918. Self awarded the French Croix-de-Guerre at Ypres and recommended for a commission. Returned to England for same September 1918 after three years and one month on active service'.

Maintaining law and order at the XL Stores, Lias Road, Porthcawl, in the late 1920s.

Coastguard John David and Police Sergeant Hugh Pritchard with Lada Niva four-wheel drive Coastguard vehicle, John Street, Porthcawl, 20 May 1990.

The staff of the post office, John Street, Porthcawl, c. 1901. From left to right, back row: -?-, -?-, Grandpa Prescott, Gronow, -?-. Centre row: -?-, Mrs Orchard, Mr I. Orchard (postmaster), May Jenkins, -?-. Front row: -?-, Dennis Orchard, -?-. Note the pill-box hats worn by the telegraph boys which were characteristic of their occupation. The original post office for Porthcawl, opened c. 1871, was located on the corner of John Street and Well Street on the site now occupied by Sidoli's Ice Cream Parlour and Restaurant. The sub-postmaster at 'Porth Cawl', as it was spelt in 1880, was a Mr George Holmes Saunders. In that year, to quote from *Slater's Directory of South Wales*: 'Letters from all parts arrive (from Bridgend) at seven in the morning and one in the afternoon, and are despatched thereto at fifteen minutes past three in the afternoon and forty-five past five in the evening'. The post office was also the money order and telegraph office and savings bank. Post-boxes at Newton and Nottage were cleared at half-past five in the evening, except on Sundays. George Saunders was still the sub-postmaster in 1884. By 1901, *Kelly's Directory of South Wales* recorded that this appointment was now classed as postmaster and was filled by Mr I. Orchard.

Porthcawl fire brigade, 1933. From left to right: back row: W. David, Dan Hopkin, David J. Hopkin, O. Howe, ? James, W. Lewis, M. Jenkins, T. Packwood, W. Farrow. Front row: W. Roberts, A. James, W.J. Farrow, E. John, F. Rowe.

Council members outside the Council offices in John Street for the Silver Jubilee of King George V and Queen Mary, 1935. When the Coliseum cinema was built and opened *c.* 1910, rooms on its first floor were leased as a council chamber and offices with the first council meeting being held there on 15 January 1912. From left to right, front row: bugler, Inspector Davies, Mr George Beynon, Cllr Thomas (at rear), Mr Gwyn Jenkins (Clerk to the Council – a part-time officer until April 1950 when the appointment was made full-time), Mr Arthur Rees (Surveyor), Chairman Jenkin Philips, Cllr Louglin Paper, -?-, Mr Chalk, Mr T.G. Jones, -?-, bugler, Mr Walker (Gas Manager). In the doorway: Cllr Thomas (builder), Cllr Tom Richards, Mr C. Chorley, -?-, Mr Theodore Burnell.

Porthcawl Urban District Council, 1956-57 showing the Chairman for that year, Cllr Tom Matthias, councillors and staff.

The old Porthcawl Urban District Council offices, South Road, Porthcawl being demolished in May 1977. The house had been leased for council offices in April 1936 and purchased in May 1944. Following the reorganisation of the Glamorgan County boundaries in 1974, the Porthcawl Town Council moved to new premises in Victoria Avenue.

Members of the Porthcawl Round Table at their annual dinner, 1974.

Porthcawl and Pyle Boy Scouts Association at a local occasion in Pen-y-Fai, near Bridgend, c. 1926. From left to right, back row: Mr Herbert Mabley (Cub Master), Mr Bill Jones (Scout Master), Mr Fred Ashton, Mr Neville White, Mr Harris, Mr Leslie Lee. Front row: Mr Miles Miles (Bridgend Assistant Commissioner), Mr J.P. Hayes (Commissioner), Mr George McCrackan (District Scout Master).

The Porthcawl branch of the Girl Guides in the late 1920s.

Porthcawl Sea Cadets, 1978. The unit changed its name to TS St David in 1979. From left to right, back row: S. Street, ? Cox, G. Hill, ? Dyer, -?-. Centre row: A. Davies, ? Gadd, ? Edwards, C. Wilkins. Front row: A.K. Jones, R.C. Jones, ? Tombes, ? , R. Davies, S. Williams, ? Phillips.

Retiring Commanding Officer, Angus Walker, with Porthcawl Nautical Girls Training Corps, 1978.

Members of the Porthcawl Army Cadets, winners of Porthcawl's Army, Navy and Cadet Services, pictured with the Mayor of Porthcawl, Cllr Matthews, 1956-57.

Cadets of No. 2347 (Porthcawl) Squadron Air Training Corps at RAF Lyneham in 1969. Squadron Leader Rennie Davies is standing on the left of the Station Commander who is in battledress.

Nine

Views and Scenery

The sea-front at Porthcawl looking towards the Seabank Hotel, *c.* 1910.

The Green, Porthcawl, just after the turn of the century. Note the bandstand on the left of the photograph.

Looking out over Rest Bay with the Porthcawl Rest Home in the distance, *c.* 1914.

The Promenade, Porthcawl, showing the old shelter, *c.* 1910.

A very young Sabrina Malvisi on the lower promenade, Porthcawl, in the mid-1940s.

Cosy Corner, Porthcawl, showing the skating rink, mid-1930s.

Cosy Corner, Porthcawl, viewed from the air in the 1930s.

The old man of the sea, *c.* 1933. This curious figure was once to be seen in the garden of a cottage in Poplar Road, Porthcawl. A ship's figurehead, it originally graced the prow of the barque, *William Miles*, which went aground on Sandy Bay in 1883. Old inhabitants who remembered the incident, recalled that the vessel was not a storm-driven victim of the sea; on the contrary, the night was fine when the ship foundered and for some unaccountable reason, she drifted ashore and was never refloated. Eventually, the barque broke up and its figurehead was carried off to be re-erected in a garden. Here, it became a bogey-man to children and a figure with which those 'worse for wear' would carry on a one-sided argument. Some years ago, the figurehead was sadly destroyed on a bonfire because it had begun to rot away.

A fairly recent photograph of Jennings Warehouse on the harbour at Porthcawl during an exceptionally high tide.

Stoneleigh House, Porthcawl, at the turn of the century. Originally a private house, by 1910 this had become a school for young ladies run by the Brills. The programme for the pageant play held at Nottage Court on 20 July 1910, records that Fraülein Brill provided pupils from Stoneleigh Cottage, Porthcawl, to be the morris dancers. In due course, the house became Victoria's night-club, but is now unoccupied.

Camping at Trecco Bay in the 1920s.

Beach Road, Newton, *c.* 1930.

Rhych Avenue, Newton, 1931. One of the many photographs taken by a young Janet Loveluck who as part of her itinerary from the mouth of the River Ogmore to Porthcawl, recorded for posterity, many landmarks in the besanded area between these two points as well as the old harbour works at Porthcawl.

Nottage village, in the mid-1930s.

Elm Tree Cottage, Nottage. This is the only building in the village to be registered as an ancient monument. In a survey carried out by Sir Cyril Fox in the late 1920s, he recorded that this was the oldest property in Nottage.

Ten

Events

The programme of the pageant play held at Nottage Court on 19 and 20 July 1910. A seven-page document, it has proved to be a mine of information for confirming the names of people, their occupations and places of residence at this time. The event was held in aid of the building fund for All Saints' Church, the foundation stone of which was eventually laid by George Edward Blundell on 7 August 1912.

The ecclesiastical procession in the pageant play at Nottage Court in 1910. The cardinal was played by the Revd T.J. Davies and the bishops by Mr Elcock and Mr Kappel. They were accompanied by canopy bearers, train bearers and acolytes, as well as priests played by Messrs David Morgan, Oliver and Rees, and monks by Messrs Fred Evans, Hopkins, Jones, Kingdom, Moyle and Wood. There was also a court procession made up of nobles, court ladies, pages and men-at-arms. All in all, it was an event in which everyone appears to have taken part!

Miss Kate Henry was one of the court ladies who took part in the court procession in the pageant play at Nottage Court, 1910.

The *Speedwell* lifeboat and crew being pulled by a team of horses through Newton village and past the schoolroom during Mabsant celebrations, *c.* 1885.

Welfare clinic outing at Nottage, 1928. Fred H. Rees is the young boy (about 5 years old) holding his hat and standing in front of the two ladies on the far right of the group.

The scene at Nottage Well during a summer drought in the mid-1930s when it was necessary to collect water for the cows. Among those pictured are J.A. Rees (boy left-hand side), Betty Williams, Joyce Lewis, Kenny Davies, Brenda Rees (girl next to pump), Philip Howells.

Opening of Porthcawl's promenade, 1935. As reported in the local press: 'Another Step in the Resort's Progress. Porthcawl's rapid advance during the past decade to a place among the leading watering places of Wales was carried a step further on Thursday when the town's fine double-decker promenade, extending along the centre of the sea-front, was formally opened in the presence of leading Glamorgan public men and representatives of industry, and thousands of holiday-makers'. Cllr Jenkin Phillips JP, Chairman of Porthcawl Urban District Council began the ceremonies by cutting the ribbon at the northern end of the new £15,000 promenade. The photograph shows Cllr Phillips walking the lower-deck promenade after the opening. From left to right: Mr Gwyn Jenkins, Mrs Phillips, Chairman Mr Jenkin Phillips and members of Porthcawl Urban District Council. Porthcawl's sea-front was given another face-lift when the new promenade was opened by the Mayor of Ogwr, Cllr Richard Power on 8 April 1995.

Mary Davies, the carnival queen, with her retinue in the Porthcawl ambulance procession during Porthcawl's second Carnival, *c.* 1936. The photograph was taken in the Winter Gardens at the Grand Pavilion. From left to right: Kathleen Beere, Beryl Morgan, Jean Harris, Pauline Oliver, Josie Carpenter, June Colwill, Marion James, Derick Harris, Mary Davies.

Carnival float on the back of a lorry in the 1930s. From left to right, standing: Margaret Callister, Reg Sampson, Peggy Bryant, ? Denham, Mary Beere, Tegid Main, Joan Howells, Leslie Roberts, John Clare, John Newman. Seated: Kenneth Hamil, Pam Cameron, Joan Lewis. The person standing by the rear of the lorry and the driver are unknown.

Carnival float, 1935. From left to right, standing: Betty Roberts, Alma Evans, -?-, -?-. Sitting: Vivian House, Carol Evans, Pauline Oliver, Megan Roberts. Fairy: Shelia Phillips. Page boys: Lesley Martin, Malcolm Stradling. The king and queen are unfortunately anonymous.

Coach outing from the New Inn (now The Sea Horse) public house, South Road, in the 1930s. The landlord, Mr Bill Witcher is on the left with his wife, Mrs Witcher, fourth from left. Others in the group are: George Evans, Charles Allen, Evan McTiffin, Haydn McTiffin, Eddie McTiffin, Bryn Llewellyn, Monty Jones, Billy David, Randall Thomas, ? Ashman, Bryn Rogers and ? Rowe.

Porthcawl's first Round Table carnival, July 1959.

Porthcawl Horticultural Society annual show, August 1981. The green-fingered Tinkler family gained the prizes for the 'Most Points in Show', the 'Most Points in Vegetables', the 'Best in Show' and the 'Best Vegetables'. From left to right: Mrs Audrey Tinkler, Dr Geoffrey Tinkler, Mrs Christine Tinkler and Master Rhidian Tinkler.

Group assembled in front of St John the Baptist Church at Newton to celebrate the Coronation of Queen Elizabeth II, 1953. From left to right, front row: Dilwyn Taylor, Alan Kingdom, Carol Matthews, David Deere, -?-, Guy Jones, ? Baker, Christine Baker, Sheila Hart, Rosemary Andrews, Barry Thomas, -?-, Terry Davies. Second row: Jean Thomas (daughter of Mrs Jean Thomas), Miss Williams, -?-, Lynne Frost, Diana Brooks, Mr Elcock, Mrs L.E. Deere (councillor), Mr R.P.T. Deere (Chairman of Porthcawl Urban District Council), Siân Jones, -?-, Eleanor Williams, Allan Hart, Jill Frost, -?-, -?-. Third row: -?-, Mrs Andrews, -?-, Mrs Davies (School House), Mrs E. Kingdom, Winnie Williams, Mrs Thomas, Mrs Elcock, Mrs Myrtle Taylor, Mrs Packwood, Anne Shell, Mrs Hart, Nancy Kingdom. Back row: Pam Thomas, Thelma Taylor, Betty Williams, Mrs Beatie Williams, Mrs Jeff Morgan.

Queen's Avenue, Porthcawl, following the big snowstorm of 1947.

'The blizzard', Porthcawl, Saturday, 9 January 1982. The author is pictured here watching the exodus of the Australian rugby team from the Seabank Hotel. The blizzard brought a bizarre climax to their 1981-82 tour of the British Isles. The Wallabies were due to turn out against the Barbarians at the National Stadium, Cardiff, on Saturday, 9 January 1982, but on that morning there was more than a foot of snow covering the pitch. Drifts on the terraces were much deeper and with further snow forecast, the game was cancelled. This was just as well as Porthcawl was cut off by the snow and the Wallabies would not have been able to reach Cardiff anyway. In the end, a number of helicopters were hired and the Wallabies were flown out in groups from the Green in front of the Seabank Hotel where they had been staying overnight.

Another scene from the blizzard that struck Porthcawl in January 1982. The 'miracle of little Snowdrop' was the caption used by the *Glamorgan Gazette* with this photograph. Farmer Edgar Evans of West Road, Nottage, found this little waif in a sheltered corner of a field on his Springfield Farm at about seven o'clock on the Saturday morning. When discovered, the calf was covered in icicles almost hanging down to the ground; the little creature was extremely lucky to be alive. The calf was covered with a polythene bag for three days to help her thaw out and sweat to keep warm. Visible from West Road, the cows and calf could not move from their sheltered corner of the field for seven days.

The morning after the fire which gutted Hockings Toy and Gift Shop on the corner of John Street and Well Street, c. 1984.

'Night-club gutted in major blaze'. The Stoneleigh Club, Porthcawl, as captured by the *Glamorgan Gazette* photographer following the fire which completely burnt out the building on Tuesday, 5 September 1989. Porthcawl's best known night-spot was destroyed and adjoining premises severely damaged as a result of the fire. It took more than 70 firemen with 11 appliances from all three Glamorgan fire services to bring the blaze under control. The fire was first spotted by a passing policeman at 1.03 a.m. in the morning and he immediately raised the alarm. It was only at 7.59 a.m., after six hours continuous effort by the fire-fighters, that the fire was finally extinguished. They had used seven water-jets, six hose-reels and two water towers in their struggle to control the fire during which four firemen received minor injuries. The burnt-out shell of the club remained an eyesore for many years until it was finally demolished on 24 April 1992.

Eleven

War Years

The author on holiday in Porthcawl during the Second World War, with his mother Mrs Marjorie Morgan, sister, Pauline, and grandmother, Mrs Henrietta Munkley. From Newton-Nottage Road, it was, in those days, a fairly short and uninterrupted walk to the sand dunes on Newton Burrows where this photograph was taken. It was not possible to continue to the beaches at either Sandy Bay or Trecco because of the barbed wire strung along the top of the dunes as an anti-invasion defence.

Troops camping at Rest Bay, Porthcawl, in the early 1900s. Between 1899 and 1902 British forces were involved in a protracted Imperial struggle with the Boers of South Africa. The photograph is on the front of a 'giant card per half-penny post'. This was sent to Miss Nellie Trollope in Swansea and bears a King Edward VII half-penny stamp franked in Porthcawl at 10 a.m. on 10 August, 1908.

Troops marching down John Street, Porthcawl, returning from South Africa after the end of the Boer War, c. 1902. The middle group of soldiers are wearing Australian-style hats with the side brim turned up. Note that some of the buildings were originally designed as domestic properties prior to the conversion of most of them to shops. Even though shop-fronts have now been added to them all, these buildings can still be recognised today from their distinctive upper stories with Victorian-style gables.

Confident nurses and soldiers examining what must have been a defused and disarmed First World War mine washed ashore at Rest Bay. From 1915 onwards, until the end of the war, the Porthcawl Rest was run by the St John Ambulance Association as an auxiliary war hospital. During this period, almost 2,500 casualties from the British, Australian, New Zealand and Canadian forces were treated and cared for at The Rest.

The Army (possibly the 15th Battalion of the Welch Regiment) camping in fields at Ty Coch Farm, *c.* 1937.

Where are they now? The Porthcawl Red Cross during the Second World War. From left to right, back row: Mrs Tydvil Morgan, Miss Edna Morgan, Mrs Neeta Jenkins, Mrs R. Oliver, Miss Bronwen Hughes, Miss Elena Green, Mrs C. Richards, Miss D. Evans, Miss Lucy Harding, Miss Wilcock, Miss Thomas, Ms N.S. Wilson, Miss Harris, Miss Beryl Davey, Miss Cassie Jones. Middle row: Miss Vandell, Miss Lil Thomas, Mrs Gwyneth Williams, Mrs Eileen Downe, Ms Norah Dyke, Mrs Daisy Longman, Miss B. Smith, Miss Norah Wood, Ms M. Hodge, Miss Ruby Stoot, Miss V. Hillie, Miss Q. Willie, Ms R. Probert, Mrs N. Styles. Front row: Mrs N. Williams, Mrs Evelyn Rees, Mrs Gwen Powell AM, Mrs Wilfred Evans (Lady Superintendent), Mrs Chalke (Commandant), Miss Katie James (Secretary), Mrs Kate Rees, Miss Nellie Dick, Miss Boucher.

Porthcawl Home Guard on parade, in Picton Avenue, during the Second World War. From left to right, first rank: -?-, Mr Benson, Mr T. Payne, -?-, -?-, Mr W. Bryant, Mr Ashbridge, Mr McCracken and Mr McEwan.

Mr Horace Walter ('Curly') Brown posing in his Home Guard uniform at the back of Queen's Avenue with son, Peter Henry William, and daughter, Elizabeth, in the early 1940s.

Air crew with Whitley bomber at RAF Stormy Down about 1942.

A Westland Wallace with ground crew near the hangar at RAF Stormy Down, 1939-40. This two-seat biplane was used for target-towing practice until superseded in later years by the Westland Lysander. The plane towed a target drogue at which pursuing aircraft fired with their bullets dipped in either red or blue paint. The coloured holes in the drogue would be used after the exercise for identification purposes in recording successful hits.

Ground crew with Fairey Battle, RAF Stormy Down, 1940.

Not all plain sailing! A crashed Handley-Page Hamden Mk.I bomber at RAF Stormy Down on 23 April 1940. This aircraft, Serial No L4042 of 16 OTU, 6 Group, and piloted by Pilot Officer C.J.R. Walker, crash- landed on Newton Down following its return from an air firing practice flight. There was no concrete landing strip at Stormy Down; the aeroplanes landed on the grass. On this occasion, it had been raining and visibility was bad; the brakes proved to be ineffective and the aircraft overshot the grass 'runway'. Fortunately, there were no casualties.

An Air Sea Rescue Marine Craft Unit was stationed at Porthcawl throughout the Second World War to provide a rescue service for ditched air craft and other distress situations. The unit operated from Porthcawl's outer harbour and used Jennings Warehouse for servicing the boats. It was at this time that the slipway was significantly improved to enable these fairly large 37-foot-long marine craft to be drawn up into the building.

RAF Sunderland flying boat off Porthcawl breakwater, 1949. During the Second World War, the Sunderlands were based in Pembroke Dock from where they carried out shore and anti-submarine patrols of the Bristol Channel and the western approaches to the British Isles from the Atlantic Ocean. The Short Sunderland S.25 was a formable craft, nicknamed 'The Flying Porcupine' by the German Luftwaffe because of the numerous machine guns that it carried.

'Off to the bank', 1941. It was business as usual at the Seabank Hotel, Porthcawl, during the early days of the Second World War. Not long after this photograph of Miss Enid Endicott and Miss Gwyneth Jenkins was taken, the Seabank Hotel was commandeered by the Army for military purposes and all the staff lost their jobs. Prior to that time, the Seabank was a very popular place with plenty of guests staying there. The hotel was owned by a Mr Pope and managed jointly by a Mr Schmit and his French wife. During 1940, two well known people stayed at the hotel. One was Prince Bernard of the Netherlands, who came to inspect the Dutch troops stationed at Dan-y-Graig; the other was film star David Niven, who was a colonel in the Army and, it is assumed, was stationed for a time in Porthcawl with his regiment.

DUKWs at Coney Beach following the end of the Second World War. These ex-American army amphibious craft were ideal for providing pleasure trips out into the sea off Sandy Bay. Examples of these vehicles can mostly be seen now with preservation societies, although there are still two in continuous use in St Helier, Jersey, where they are used for conveying passengers to and from Elizabeth Castle in St Aubin's Bay.

The Second World War pill-box at the breakwater end of the promenade, Porthcawl, 19 February 1989. Sadly this relic of the last war was covered up when the promenade was refurbished in 1995. Note the 'traffic lights' on the top of the watch tower which are used by ships navigating Porthcawl harbour.

A poignant scene at Porthcawl cemetery and a grim reminder of the Second World War. Some of the graves of airmen from RAF Stormy Down who died in the service of their country bear witness to the waste of human life in war. Members of the British, Polish and Commonwealth air forces are buried in this cemetery.

Graves of sailors of the Second World War at Porthcawl cemetery. Perhaps the most moving headstones from any conflict, are those which bear the inscription 'Known only to God'.

Twelve

Sport

Who put the 'Royal' into Porthcawl? HRH Edward, Prince of Wales with officials and members of the Royal Porthcawl Golf Club, 1932. The Prince was Patron here from 1923 until 1936, the year of his abdication. The rare privilege of using the prefix 'Royal' was obtained, however, on 30 March 1909, a long time before the Prince became the club's Patron. The Porthcawl Golf Club, itself, was formed in 1891 by a group of Cardiff businessmen. Mrs Gordon of Nottage Court and members of the Easter Vestry in April of the same year, granted the club's founders permission to use Lock's Common as a golf course. However, not fully satisfied with their first efforts to establish a suitable course on the Common, the club decided to move to its present location. The clubhouse on this site, which is considered to be one of the best natural sites for a golf course anywhere in the world, was officially opened by Mrs Ebsworth on 6 May 1899.

The ladies at the Royal Porthcawl Golf Club in the early 1900s. The first recorded competition for ladies was a nine-hole medal played on 4 November 1894. This was won by a Mrs Earle who also went on to carry off the December medal in the same year.

The clubhouse at Royal Porthcawl with the Rest Home in the background. This photograph was taken in the 1930s and alterations have subsequently been carried out to the clubhouse.

A young Anne Proudfoot at Nottage Halt, 22 May 1961. This halt was demolished in 1964 following the closure of the Porthcawl branch railway line. The station at Nottage, built in 1897, became popularly known as 'Golfers' Halt' after it came into use in March of the following year. Those golfers alighting from the trains who did not wish to walk from the station, could be transported to the club (at a fee) by horse-drawn carriages which met each train.

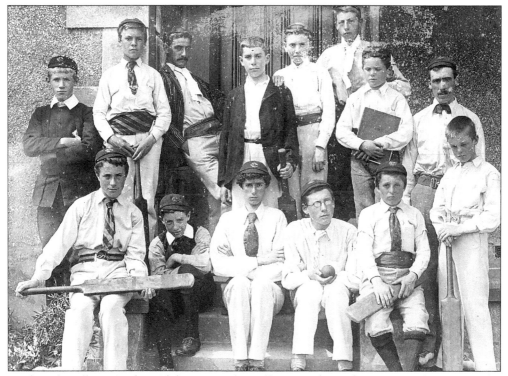

Porthcawl College Cricket Club, 1896. The college was housed in Sea Bank House – the Brogden's old residence. From left to right, back row: H. Gibson, R. Fletcher, J. Towns, C.F. Biggs (Captain), W.R. Evans, C. Crossley, R. Gibson, R. Elias. Front row: H.G. Smith, C.F. Rowlands, T. David, H. Rankin, G. Deer, W.C. Bollerill.

Porthcawl Cricket Club in the 1920s.

Newton Association Football Club, 1924-25 season during which they won 24 out the 36 games played, drew 6 and lost 6. From left to right, back row: David Thomas, -?-, -?-, Bertie Williams, -?-, -?-, George Roberts, 'Old Mr Pinchin'. Middle row: Ray Longman, Bobbie Jacks, -?-, -?-, Lyn Hull, Rees Griffiths, Mr Charlie Davies. Front row: Brynley Thomas, Harry Pinchin, Eddie Williams.

Porthcawl United Association Football Club, 1948-49. The club was started by Fred Warmington and Henry Williams who are standing left and right at the ends of the back row.

Porthcawl Rugby Football Club, 1935-36.

Porthcawl Men's Bowling Club playing at home against a visiting team from Epsom, 1953.

The Porthcawl Ladies Bowling Club in the 1950s.

Thirteen

Entertainment and Leisure

Paul Robeson (1898-1976), famous American singer, civil rights activist and 'honorary Welshman' The links between Paul Robeson and South Wales were first forged in 1928 when he listened to a group of Rhondda miners who had marched to London to voice their plight. Robeson identified a link between the miners' harsh conditions and those of his fellow black-Americans back home. He promised to visit South Wales at the end of the record-breaking production of *Showboat*, in which he was then starring at the Drury Lane Theatre, London. True to his word, Robeson visited the mining valleys on a number of occasions, developing strong links and a special relationship with the area. In 1939, he made a film called *The Proud Valley* in which he took the part of a black stoker who helps unemployed Welsh miners re-open their pit. Persecuted in his own country under the McCarthy 'reign of terror' and unable to leave America, Robeson, as a guest of honour, broadcast via a transatlantic telephone link, singing Ar hyd y nos and other songs to the audience at the Miners' Eisteddfod being held at the Grand Pavilion at Porthcawl. For such reasons, Paul Robeson earned himself a place in the history of the Welsh mining communities.

Long before the Grand Pavilion was built in Porthcawl, entertainment was provide by the likes of the Porthcawl Orchestra shown here about 1895. From left to right, back row: Mr Ben Rowe, -?-, Mr William Simpson, Mr David Hutchinson. Front row: Mrs Martha Walters (*née* Sampson), Mr Richard Sampson, Mrs Tom Jackson (*née* Pearce), Mrs Lily Mack (*née* Sampson). The Sampsons ran a well known ironmongery emporium on Station Hill.

Building the dome of the Grand Pavilion, Porthcawl, 1932. George Matthews, master carpenter and works engineer, is standing second from the left. The Grand Pavilion was the brainchild of Russell Mabley, one of Porthcawl's outstanding civic leaders. When he was elected a member of Porthcawl Urban District Council in 1925, Russell Mabley was the youngest ever councillor to serve on the local council. He repeated this feat by becoming the youngest ever chairman when he was elected as Porthcawl's chief citizen in 1931. Costing £21,000 to build, the official opening of the Grand Pavilion took place on 12 August 1932. Recording that important occasion, the *Glamorgan Gazette*'s headline was 'Porthcawl's March Onward'. Architecturally, the design of the Grand Pavilion was very advanced for its time, the most conspicuous feature being the huge octagonal dome. With its concert hall and extensive Winter Gardens, it was considered to be a mecca for entertainment and dancing. The use of reinforced concrete, then a fairly new concept for building, had been used in its construction. The Grand Pavilion has had a colourful history ever since and has recently received a major face-lift to bring it up to an even higher standard of excellence as an entertainment centre.

The ventriloquist, Valentine Vox and friend. This was typical of the acts presented in the Grand Pavilion during the 1930s.

The South Sea Island girls of Porthcawl Operatic Society in their performance of *South Pacific* at the Grand Pavilion in 1973.

One of the major events in the holiday-makers' calendar, was the bathing beauty contest. As the 1977 poster states, contests were to be held every Wednesday in the Grand Pavilion to elect a weekly winner who would be invited to attend a grand final at the end of the season to elect a 'Miss Porthcawl'.

A selection of bathing beauties parading for the photographer on the promenade at Porthcawl prior to taking part in the contest. This shot would have been taken some time after 1972 when Dunraven Court, in the background, was built. This building was demolished in 1996.

The Casino cinema, Porthcawl, now showing the well-known box office hit, *The Sound of Music*. One of Julie Andrews' greatest successes, the film still receives a regular airing on television, usually over the Christmas holiday period. The Casino was closed as a cinema in 1974 to become the Stoneleigh night-club.

Another of Porthcawl's cinemas was the Coliseum in John Street which closed its doors in May 1968. The building is now occupied by a supermarket. As a holiday resort, all the latest films were shown in Porthcawl. This can be seen from the newspaper clipping taken from the *Glamorgan Gazette* of Friday, 1 June 1951, where the heart-throbs of the period, Stewart Granger and Deborah Kerr, were starring at the Casino in *King Solomon's Mines*.

CASINO
PORTHCAWL

FOR ONE WEEK   JUNE 4
OUTSTANDING ATTRACTION
STEWART   DEBORAH
GRANGER   KERR
RICHARD CARLSON In
RIDER HAGGARD'S

KING SOLOMON'S MINES

Filmed in Technicolour in Africa
Screened at 6.5 and 8.45
Also
FULL SUPPORTING
PROGRAMME

COLISEUM
PORTHCAWL

MON. TUES. WED.   JUNE 4, 5, 6
BURT   JOANNE
LANCASTER   DRU
SALLY FORREST in

VENGEANCE ALLEY

also Barry Sullivan Arlene Dahl in
INSIDE THE STRAIGHT

THURS. FRI. SAT.   JUNE 7, 8, 9
JANE WYMAN   VAN JOHNSON
HOWARD KEEL   BARRY SULLIVAN in

3 Guys Named Mike

Also
James Whitmore Nancy Davies in
THE NEXT VOICE YOU HEAR

Children in the paddling pool on Porthcawl front in the 1920s. The Grand Pavilion, not built until 1932, is conspicuous by its absence.

The Salt Lake bathing pool, Porthcawl, in the 1920s. Jennings Warehouse is on the far right of the photograph. Following its decline as a port, the entrance to the old inner basin of the harbour was bricked up about 1926, creating a lagoon which became known as the Salt Lake. Over the years, the lake became very popular with swimmers and for boating. The whole area was filled in during the Second World War to become an American Army vehicle park in 1943 and later a large coach and car park.

Coney Beach, Porthcawl, in the 1930s. The funfair was built on the site of an old tip where the ballast from incoming ships to Porthcawl had been dumped over many years. It was started with two surplus First World War aircraft hangars which can be seen to the centre of the photograph.

'Some things never change'. The Waite sisters of Kenfig Hill, Cassie on the left and Janet on the right, fussing over the ponies on Sandy Bay, August 1930. Miss Cissie John, also of Kenfig Hill, is standing second from the right. Donkeys and ponies remain a big attraction on the beach to this day.

Llynfi caravan site, West Road, Nottage. The site first started before the Second World War with campers erecting tents in the orchard behind Llynfi House. It was later turned into a caravan site when a licence was obtained by Mr Sid Gibbons. It eventually came under the ownership of Mr Tom Jones, in the centre of the above panoramic view, until sold in 1983 to make way for a housing development.

Sid Herbert's caravan camp at Newton in the early 1930s, on the site of Bryneglwys Gardens.

'The Travel People'. Over the years, leisure and holiday habits have greatly changed. Even though Porthcawl still heaves at the seams during the summer months, holidays abroad are now within the grasp of many more people. A typical example of a local firm that caters for these needs is that of Traveland, owned and run by Carol and Phillip George.

The narrow gauge railway, Porthcawl, in the 1930s. This miniature railway ran from Coney Beach alongside the Eastern Promenade to the end of the Salt Lake at Cosy Corner. It was of great delight to passengers especially if you were lucky enough to go through the small tunnel on the slip line. This railway has sadly gone, but today the clock has turned a full circle and we now have the *Promenade Princess*, the new Green Road train that follows the same route as part of its journey from Sandy Bay to Rest Bay and back.

Family fun on the Porthcawl miniature railway in the late 1950s. From left to right: Miss Malvina Angell (with back to camera), Mrs Marjorie Morgan, Mrs Henrietta Munkley, Miss Shân Morgan, Miss Elaine Jenkins, Master John Jenkins, Miss Pauline Morgan.